HABIT KICKS AND LAUGHTER

Marc Corn

Habit, Kicks and Laughter

Marc Corn

Other Books By Marc Corn

Moral Rat: The First Edition

Credits

I would like to thank each person who has helped bring this book to light. Who knew my crazy ideas could become reality?

Well now we know you can achieve anything, even if your the craziest person in the world.

Why Write This Book?

I guess you could say I have a lot of time on my hands just to moan about subjects that people are ashamed to talk about, or it's just because I am a boring individual who has nothing else better to do.

You Decide!

Talking with Your Mouthful
1.

When we were younger our parents taught us how not to talk with our mouthful with the intention of teaching us how not to share your food with everyone around you! What is so difficult? Insert food, chew it up with your mouth closed and swallow.

So, what makes the human mind forget this routine when someone talks to you? The prevailing-opinion is that it's just bad manners and people who do it are just really rude. According to my research, people forget that food is in their mouth and therefor showing the contents of their mouth or spraying everyone in their direction with food.

Let's think, how you could prevent this from happening? Easy, just think about what your doing. I know it could be hard for some people, distractions from Mobile Phones, Computers and Televisions can cause their focus to be diverted from the task in hand.

So, your in a situation where someone is talking with their mouthful and you want them to stop, do you tell them or would you leave it to spare their feelings? Depending on your own personality it might not phase you to say "Hey stop talking with your mouthful" and not take any concern of other people's feelings. But most of the time people are very reluctant to say anything to spare their feelings or cause a scene.

The best thing you can do is be civil about it and just look the other way, some people may get the urge to say something and be rude about it but as the old say goes, "Out of Sight, Out of Mind".

Just Look The Other Way...

Scratching Your Butt
2.

Got an itch? Just scratch it, right? But is it still acceptable when the itch is located on you're butt? Scratching yourself near an area that excretes rejected waste is very disgusting.

For many years it has been widely known that men scratch their backsides and not really care where or when they do it. Some men adopt the attitude of "Needs Must", meaning if you got an itch just scratch it.

So, men are labeled the ultimate butt scratchers but what about women? Surely they give their rumps a scratch from time to time. There will be many women who will deny they scratch themselves, let alone their backside's, not very lady as they say. Women have been known to scratch their backside's but they do it discretely and then deny doing it in fear of not being seen as not lady like.

Face facts, everyone does it! You can't hide the fact that there hasn't been at least one time you have had to scratch your backside, it's only a natural reaction after all.

Scratching your backside may seem disgusting but sometimes the urge can become too much but remember, if you decide to scratch your backside then wash your hands after or invest in a butt scratcher.

Nagging 3.

So, you're sitting on the sofa and someone comes in nagging at you to do something, all you want to do is relax on the sofa, its a constant drone, switch off and agree from time to time, easy that way.

We all like to have a nag, both men and women, it's not an all female profession. The availing opinion is that women nag the most and go out their way just to do it, men think that all women come with a built in nag radar that is constantly on the go, do men forget they nag too?

We hate it. They hate it. So why do we do it? Most of the time we nag the ones we love or those we try to encourage to do better for themselves, it is because we care for those people.

Some forms of nagging can really do harm, depending on the person it could really annoy and alienate them to the point where they will want to ignore you or even scream and shout at you. There is only so much a person can take before they say "enough is enough".

Fact is we all do it, both men and women. So, next time you are being nagged remember you probably do it too!

Whining

4.

Whining, we all do it, and frankly if you think you don't then stop kidding yourself. If you look at your own daily activities there will be something that will make you whine and even though you protest it gets done, just with a lot of swearing and mumbling.

When we were younger it was probably a sure thing that whining was a daily occurrence, obviously being of a young age our level of understanding wasn't great and every activity would cause us to whine.

Being adults you would think we would of grown out of that stage but alas that isn't the case, in reality some people actually get worse as they get older. There is no excuse for you to use your childhood to hide bad behaviors and negative traits.

There is only one way to stop you from whining, at every point you feel like having a whinge just take a deep breath and take it in your stride.
If you still feel the urge to whinge then you have no hope, just suck it up and get on with it because the world won't wait for you.

Don't allow yourself to become wrapped up in a circle of whining, even though we all do it from time to time its still no excuse to waste your just whining about pointless activities.

Body Odor
5.

Each of us suffer with body odor at some point in our life, nothing to be embarrassed about it's a natural body reaction. People don't realize that there are many causes of body odor; some medical, weight and others due to daily activities.

The one thing I noticed during my research is that people hate it when others don't wash, either because they can't be bothered or just pure laziness. Picture yourself in this situation; Your on a tube train, its packed to the rafters and your standing holding onto the over head bar, and then you suddenly smell something bad, you realize it is the person next you, what do you do? Look the other way? Hold yor nose?

There are many ways you can prevent body odor; washing regular, pay close attention to areas prone to sweating, change your cloths regularly and use a good antiperspirant.

If your someone who can't be bothered to control body odor then honestly you need to get out of that train of thought, being a stinky bugger isn't really an attractive quality, also it's not hygienic and can make you feel run down if it is left for any length of time.

Unless you have a medical condition, you have no excuse not to wash. So, get in the shower and don't be a stinky minx!

Compulsive Household Rearranger
6.

Compulsive household rearranging, how annoying this can be! In every home everything has it's place and we become stuck in a routine, expecting everything to be in it's place.

There are many people who suffer with OCD(obsessive compulsive-disorder) and have different compulsive traits. Moving furniture or objects is one of the most common forms of OCD, no one really knows why people do this, maybe it is a need for everything to be perfect, who knows?

Living with someone who constantly feels the urge to move everything about can be hard at times, never knowing why they do it or what triggers them to do it.

Being creatures of habit we always expect things to be in it's place and we get agitated when it's not. This can also be seen as a form of OCD as you want it to be a certain way. In reality someone with OCD is just like any normal person, creatures of habit and always seeking perfection.

Everyone seeks some form of perfection in life and in someways this can be seen as OCD. So, really everyone is the same apart from some people are labeled and others are not.

Time to ditch those labels!

Nail Bitting
7.

Feeling peckish? Why not nosh on you're finger nails! Many people bite their nails for different reasons and sometimes it's just a habit. The main causes of nail biting seems to be anxiety or hunger.

When it comes to hunger it is simply weird, why would you eat your finger nails? It isn't food after all. The worst thing is people often bite their nails after they have had a meal, some people think that this is because the person is still hungry but also it could just be a habit that happens after every meal, after all we are creatures of habit.

Nail bitting is also very common in children for the same reasons as adults, but sometimes it is just because they are curious or bored. If you want to stop someone from nail biting then there are many methods you could use, but nagging won't help, in theory it could make it worse!

The first thing you need to do is address any anxiety problems, each person has their own worries and it could be a comfort technique that they have chosen to hide any worries. If you determine that it is just a habit then simply support that person and offer your own advice, purchasing special nail varnish can also be an advisable route for both adults and children.

If the person starts to kick the habit then you will need to reassure them so that any future incidents will not occur and be twice as bad. When it comes to children it is best to nip it in the bud quickly but remember don't nag or punish, as this could make it worse and also it could take much longer for them to stop.

Get to The Point!
8.

Picture this, one of your friends comes up to you with something important to tell you, they begin by giving you a story, you sit and listen, it goes on for around 5 minutes and they still haven't got to the point, you start to think when will they get to the point.

How annoying is that situation? Why can't people just get to the point? They waste more time telling their story than just telling you what they needed to say, it's silly, save your breath and just get to the point! We don't need to hear your life story, just spit it out!

According to my research this habit mostly occurs in females, do they have more to say or do they just like talking too much? Surely this can't just be an all female problem, I know they like to talk but come on males must do it also.

Either way, do people really think we can just stand around all day listening to them jabber on? If the situation is so important then just say what it is, don't go around the houses, just get to the point, by the time you have said all that the person you are telling it to would of lost track of what your saying or they would be getting extremely bored.

There is irony within this chapter because it has taken me several hundred words just to explain the point and I can bet you any money that you have read through this thinking "Get to the point".

9. Not Washing Your Hands After Using The Toilet

Ok this one is simple, washing your hands after using the toilet, why wouldn't you wash your hands? There are so many germs in the bathroom, to be honest the problem isn't so much to do with touching your body parts, it is more to do with the germs found within the bathroom.

The practice of washing your hands after using the toilet should be taught from a young age, this would give them a healthy routine for hygiene. According to many doctors, if a child learns a good hygiene routine it will help them maintain good health as they get older.

By washing your hands it helps to rinse off the germs. All of the germs found in the bathroom are invisible to the human eye and can only be seen under a special light or microscope... When you wash your hands you need to make sure that you are using a good soap, these can be found at many retailers, if you are still lost for what soap to use then go speak with your doctor or pharmacist and they will advise you on what's best.

When I researched this subject it was concerning to read that only a small majority of the population wash their hands. There are three main factors why people don't wash their hands and they are laziness, not necessary and hypochondriac.

First of all there is no excuse, stop being lazy, it is necessary to wash your hands and lastly stop being silly. You may think it's silly but you can contract sicknesses from a toilet, it's a well known fact that people who don't wash their hands often get sick more regular.
So, no excuses, remember to wash your hands!

Passing Gas
10.

We all do it from time to time and don't you deny it! One of the big denials with passing gas is that women claim that they don't do it, when they do! Women claim to be somewhat reserved about passing gas, it's like they hold it in and go off to a secret forrest to let them rip, they must get surprised when they fart.

The biggest cause of passing wind is due to food we consume, people with diets high in dairy and unabsorbable carbohydrates usually suffer the most with wind. But you have to keep in mind that there also could be medical reasons for someone to pass gas regally.

Medical conditions can be solely responsible for someone passing wind, these conditions include:

Anxiety, Acarbose(Diabetic medication), Intestinal Disease and Constipation. Many of these conditions have similar symptoms but one of the major ones is trapped wind, which can cause a lot of pain and discomfort.

Putting aside the medical complications, passing wind is just a natural body reaction. There are many reasons why wind occurs but in a normal person wind will only occur while digesting food or swallowing air while consuming food and drinks.

Some people think that passing wind is just a disgusting habit and with most people this is true. But most of the time it's just uncontrollable and even the healthiest person has to let one go once in a while.

Farting is like success, it just bothers people.

Gossiping
11.

So, you just heard a really big rumor about someone. The rumor might not be true, but you can't keep it to yourself. You first tell one of your friends and then you go off telling the rest of your friends.
No Matter who you are, we've all done it at some point.

There are many reason's why people gossip; Boredom, Jealousy, Revenge, Control, Power, Attention, Peer Pressure or To Feel Superior. All of these are still not an excuse to gossip, before you go gossiping try to think about how the person may feel and also you don't know if the rumor is true.

Rumors can do a lot of damage, words can hurt more than people think. Believing rumors to start with can lead to bad life choices, allowing yourself to be influenced by rumors is just being dumb. If you think about it, people might be spreading the rumor but it all could be false. As the old quote goes "Would you stick you head in the oven, if they did too?".

Don't just follow what others do because it could be wrong and also being in with a crowd that does this behavior could have repercussions in later life.

Whether the rumors are true or false, everyone is entitled to privacy. The shoe would be on the other foot if the rumors were about you and I am sure you would get upset also.

Next time you hear a rumor, don't get involved. If it doesn't concern you then don't stick your nose in because in the end you will realise it's not worth it and how hurtful it can be.

Snoring

12.

Everyone denies this but chances are you do snore, no amount of denying can take it away. Before I start ripping on people who snore, let's look at the medical reasons for snoring.

There is a complete list of medical reasons why people snore and I could go on for ages explaining each one. The most common cause of snoring is sleep apnea. Sleep apnea is when a person's sleep is interrupted and they can stop breathing for a few seconds and if you don't seek medical attention it could occur repeatedly.

I hear many couples complain because their partners snore, it's really funny because they threaten to put a pillow over their partners head. Some people say their partners snoring is so loud that they sound like a warthog and keeps them awake all night.

As responsible adults you need to discuss suitable medical treatment, it will be affecting both of you and if it is left for a long period of time then it could cause other complications.

Once you find suitable medical care the problem should start to ease off and you will be able to have a peaceful nights sleep. But remember even with treatment doesn't mean it will cure the problem, after all they are only doctors and not miracle workers. I know with many conditions doctors can fix but they are only human after all.

So, resist the urge to put a pillow over someones head and work on it together to find a cure.

Ending Notes

This book wasn't made to poke fun at habits, it was more to make light of habits we all complain about. I have spent many hours researching each habit, going through hundreds of pages making sure I wouldn't cause offence by writing false information. I know there will be some people who will disagree with this book, after all you can't please everyone so you expect someone to complain.

The best thing about this book is that it will relate to you in someway and proves that each of us are connected in some small way. Even if I have made you laugh, cry or angry with this book it proves I have touched you in some way whether thats good or bad.

Legal information

Copyright © Marc Corn 2012

All Rights Reserved.
No part of this publication may be reproduced, stored in a retrieval system, or transmitted, in any form or by any means without the prior permission in writing of the publisher, nor be otherwise circulated In any form of binding or cover other than that in which it is published and without a similar condition being imposed on the subsequent purchaser.

Awareness Pictures
http://awarenesspictures.com

www.ingramcontent.com/pod-product-compliance
Ingram Content Group UK Ltd.
Pitfield, Milton Keynes, MK11 3LW, UK
UKHW041959230426
12048UKWH00008B/423